ROSA'S EINSTEIN

Camino del Sol

A Latina and Latino Literary Series

JENNIFER GIVHAN

ROSA'S EINSTEIN

POEMS

THE UNIVERSITY OF
ARIZONA PRESS
TUCSON

The University of Arizona Press
www.uapress.arizona.edu

ISBN-13: 978-0-8165-3803-4 (paper)

Cover design by Leigh McDonald
Cover art: *The Other I: The Mushroom Hunters* by Alejandra De la Torre Contreras

Publication of this book is made possible in part by the proceeds of a permanent endowment created with the assistance of a Challenge Grant from the National Endowment for the Humanities, a federal agency.

Library of Congress Cataloging-in-Publication Data are available at the Library of Congress.

Printed in the United States of America
♾ This paper meets the requirements of ANSI/NISO Z39.48-1992 (Permanence of Paper).

For Adelina Suzanne
& all las hijas wandering their own deserts

If time travel is possible, [Kurt Gödel] submitted, then time itself is impossible. A past that can be revisited has not really passed.

—"TIME BANDITS: WHAT WERE EINSTEIN & GÖDEL TALKING ABOUT?"

My life has been full of terrible misfortunes,
most of which never happened.

—MICHEL DE MONTAIGNE

There was once a poor widow who lived in a lonely cottage. She had two children like two rose-trees, one called Snow-white & the other Rose-red. The two were so fond of each other that they always held each other by the hand when they went out together, & when Snow-white said, We will not leave each other, Rose-red answered, Never so long as we live.

—THE BROTHERS GRIMM

CONTENTS

ONE

Rosa Roja   5

Lieserl Travels Back to the River, Becomes Her Mama   8

The Bomb   9

Field Trip: Lieserl Blanketed in Fallout, or Nieve   11

Un Niño, Falling   12

In the Desert Multiverse: Einstein's Single Mama   13

TWO

When the Jornada del Muerto Had a Windpipe   17

Rosa Follows Nieve into the Desert Circus   19

Lunatic Mama: The Last Hunger Artist   20

Lieserl Runs Away   22

Lieserl Reads *Goodnight Moon*   23

Lieserl Writes Her Father   24

Nieve, the Brave Sister   25

Rosa/Nieve's Sideshow Performance   26

Lieserl's Yellow   28

Lieserl Creates Light   29

Rosa & the Date Palm   30

After the Circus   31

THREE

Rosa Meets Princess Alice   35

Why Believe? or, Rosa Questions the Scientist About the Princess   37

After Meeting Princess Alice   39

Rosa Follows Lieserl into Night   40

Princess Alice Responds   41

Lieserl Contemplates Resurrection   42

The Dead Don't Crick. The Dead Believe   43

FOUR

Rosa's Time Capsule (or, Father Is a Hole & Home, a Spinning Top)   47

Risen Again   49

Accelerating Elevator   51

How to Build a Time Machine   53

Case Study: The Mexicali Border as Time Machine   54

Reinas de STEM   55

Nieve Explora   56

Rosa Dreams of Nothing   57

Ghost You Don't Believe In   58

Nieve After the Circus, Parallel   59

Rosa & Nieve Say Good-bye to the Desert Circus   60

FIVE

From the Bottom of the World Comes a Cry   63

Rosa & Nieve Grow Up   64

The World Ended. I Woke in Heaven   65

Sighting   66

River Pitch; or, Nieve Reminds Me How to Swim   67

Night After Night: Jupiter   69

Body Image; or, Nieve Reminds Me Who I Am   71

Why Are You in This World?—   73

My God, Nieve   74

Rosa & Nieve in the Beginning   75

Acknowledgments   *81*

Notes   *83*

ROSA'S EINSTEIN

ONE

ROSA ROJA

∮

It was a fool's journey from the beginning.
I knew this
though I let Lieserl

                              daughter that Einstein let go

believe anything she needed.
We'll find our father,
I know we will—

                    braiding history with myth
                    like ribbons through plaits
                    of the empty house, the cupboards bare.
                    (This isn't a fairytale, though we imagine ourselves
                              unraveling.)

I make cactus splints
for Lieserl's broken dolls
as we wander through row upon row of sunset, turning rocks
into balloon animals,
sand into melted candy, spun pink sugar.

We woke up
—that has to be the beginning.

∮

                    A man came last night.
                    Papa? Will you eat something?

Lieserl is another flora
they say was fever
dream but I've seen her, sister

in the flower-fisted garden behind the coned firs

of piñon where we pick nuts
& eat the squirrels.

Does eternity end like time in the blood?

I call out to the mad:
Papa!
—God sometimes comes in the form of a scientist—bandit
of time.

We search for water, crack the skull
of the cactus flower head
but return with every Btu of heat

                    we've never held

(nothing created
nothing destroyed).

Mama reminds me ghosts are figments
& cannot be helpful

she says, *No one knows what happened to Lieserl*—
when I read her the book, scour
the footnotes.

                    Was Mileva pressured to give her up
as Mama, me,
illegitimate daughter of broken time?

Some say she died of scarlet fever & what's left
of her belongs to pseudoscience, vanished
into the Balkan night.

Mama is a ghost.
Which is to say, she is not helpful.

I believe Lieserl fought (what daughter isn't made
for such defiance
like some brief fiery meteor?).

                    Lieserl, was it love or science
strung you like a kite? This string in my hand, this knot. Come
sister. I'll give you flight.

ƒ

LIESERL TRAVELS BACK TO THE RIVER, BECOMES HER MAMA

Full force she goes like star-tipped marigolds to the water
like blood, cold coffee, 1944: memories looping

holes in the one who sent her. He'd gone
to study science. In the eternal city she'd bear babies—

she'd use her considerable brain, will them into existence
—they'd rise like cabbages from her mama's garden

at the edge of the ridge where horses trot circles
& the Scientist taught her to stack her loves like elements,

to line them up mathematically by atomic weight, blocks
of light, blocks of wild brain chemicals, reacting.

He was gone, the Scientist who loved her badly—a violent
washing machine in her hips, tumbling. She suspects

a need for the dark memories the way mice who've lost them
in the cruel experiment return to the triangle electric though they once

knew better. (It goes away, the love, overfed & birthing time
travel. It led me to the girl in star marigolds, afloat in the water.)

THE BOMB

Sorry is my own yard.
—WILLIAM CARLOS WILLIAMS

1. LOS ALAMOS TO TRINITY

late into the night   we drank lab alcohol
      200 proof   to spice up the punch
we were young, partying   we had two dance bands
boy & girl scouts   a soda fountain & a radio station
with no call letters

a cyclotron   7,000 fire extinguishers

did I ever see a little girl white as snow
dancing in the light, blanketing
                  the light

so bright a blind woman could see her—
the child mushrooming
brain-gray shadow in the dark?

we were there for a trigger
we were there for a millionth of a second

we were there for a violent   chain reaction
that treated us for what we were:
                we were matter.

2. TRINITY SAYS

even my cows
began losing
their hair

—when it grew back
white & mottled

no two markings were alike—

lightning burn my sand into glass

your carbon bodies
my glass-boned sand

like a little girl's porcelain doll
even when shattered

is still
a doll.

FIELD TRIP: LIESERL BLANKETED IN FALLOUT, OR NIEVE

I thought Lieserl knew it was pretend—the snow
& ice exploding around us

like when she asks where we're going
I answer, *To the moon.*

It's not a trick.
That's the beauty & the grief.

When we understand that we're not going anywhere
but we go anyway.

At the nuclear museum we watched the Trinity test
the day the sun rose twice:

Nieve appeared in the mushroom cloud
above our rancho.

That's what I called her. I renamed her
Nieve, my Good Sister, favored one.

Sometimes, we pretend the extra limbs
are here to comfort us, snow-white

branches growing from our sheets
like snowflake arms in sixfold radial symmetry.

Nothing's so fragile, so perfectly shaped, as melting.

UN NIÑO, FALLING

Siempre que miro por la ventana la nieve que cae,
recuerdo mi infancia en el desierto.

Un niño, its nickname
—bomb from sandblasted bowels

New Mexican vistas overtaken in utero
delivered to Hiroshima—

shadows, y un niño, andar en bicicleta
wax on sidewalk

melted against brick
Mama breastfeeding street

ash for milk
como leche quemada

                                        Un niño

que cae
en un niño.

IN THE DESERT MULTIVERSE:
EINSTEIN'S SINGLE MAMA

In one brightly lit desert
I rebirthed Albert
& affectionately called him Bertie.

I taught him to dance cumbias
but never to catch
butterflies on their way

to Mexico neither for beauty
nor study.

He never learned
the violin & always
combed his hair.

Like me, he never had a father who never
brought home compasses
or clock parts

& we couldn't let him
wander the barrio

alone.
                        A child should know
at least one main dish so

I taught him to cook arroz con pollo
to pluck & scrub the dead bird with salt
to add one bay leaf

into the boiling red water
to bite a wooden spoon
to stop the tears of onions.

I wanted him to find
a cure for what
ailed us.

                There was never a bomb
he never accidentally
helped create.

The bomb went off.

TWO

WHEN THE JORNADA DEL MUERTO* HAD A WINDPIPE

& she was choking on deviled eggs
        with yellow mustard & paprika sprinkles
at her mama's book club picnic in the backyard

where she used to play rag dolls alone
        until she found her ghost sister
Nieve white as snow cone before the juice,

if she longed for more than salt flats
        or sand dunes or lava flows beyond the fence's
thick irrigation pipes, if she was clutching

her scarf & flailing while the mamas
        read on, pages thick with ink the color
of the crows in her dark eyes, if she was lost

& lonely but none of that mattered,
        now she was turning blue with swallowing
spongy egg pieces down the wrong tube—

I would wrap my red arms around her
        & python squeeze until she spit them out.
Maybe her mama stopped hugging her

when her father left. Maybe her mama cannot see
        her baby white sister, lightly
snowing on the desert cacti, corseting

---

   * The Jornada del Muerto (Spanish for "single day's journey of the dead one") is a desert in southern New Mexico.

cane cholla like a muted holiday wasteland.
        Maybe her mama didn't even notice
she too had almost gone away,

on the xeriscaping, not breathing nothing—
        not grown-up conversations or party cups
of pink iced lemonade or stifling

winter air. Let the desert choke.
        Let her have something inside
that nearly strangles her to tell.

Then, if she needed me to, I would reach
        inside & scrape the ridges of her burning
throat until the lump stopped growing—

if she needed me to, I would lash myself
        to her rose-colored neck, make myself a scar.

ROSA FOLLOWS NIEVE INTO THE DESERT CIRCUS

Again my ghosted sister parades herself
before sunset, glistening & sharp-toothed as
cactus rungs crackling from the red rocks
dividing the landscape into just three rings. Southwestern
elephants are shaped like bison, their white-horned skulls
framing the first act: reviving the wild dead who've
gone ahead. She's gotten so good at it—Nieve
hair like snow, Nieve tightroping white dunes of sand.
I round up the afternoon's contestants: a vulture-picked
jackalope we can tell was regal once, his crown of antlers still
knotting his temples; a scorpion mouse, our miniature
lion, night howl we're certain will return; the lunatic
mama who left us to this madness, our perpetual
necropsy in this unenchanted land where we can
only pretend. But oh, we've gotten so good at it—
performing in the center ring, two girls
quicksilver as the desert herself, where survival means
running toward the nearest cave, where
survival means imagination like water, means
tracing ourselves in the petroglyphs, chiseling our stories
under the ancients'. In the final ring, where nightfall
veins the big-top sky with starlight, hope
wears a gown of fire; turning fortune-teller, she shows us,
X-ray sharp, how this spectacle will end. Nieve
yellows into morning—she melts back into dreams, not
zombie sister, no. The real & saving thing.

LUNATIC MAMA:
THE LAST HUNGER ARTIST

after Franz Kafka

In her cage she waits
small & barred   carrying
torchlight   daring

us while we pretend not to gawk
at the porcelain

plate of her face

She must know
we cannot stand her sight
though the children

gape   amazed
Judging by the mange
we say   deranged   not right

or is she scared?
She drags her blanching
onto scattered yellow straw   strikes

a clock   She locks
the tiny glass of her lips

& sips

                    Did you mean
to let her out?

slipping
self through self
as though you were a gate.

LIESERL RUNS AWAY

Absolutely not, Mama said. *You absolutely cannot dig up Einstein*
& bring him to the circus. Ever since I was a girl I've
associated special relativity with special dark chocolate—

I've been curious. I have a secret that sounds like pieces
of silver earrings jangling against earlobes or the highest
tiny pinky key on the baby piano, better even if it's out

of tune. Through the trees, the leaves rustle, but that's not
what it sounds like, not really. When I was a virgin,
my turquoise aftertaste. I've a penchant for punching

boys in the gut, for fun, the way a vintage circus poster
is fun, before the lion escapes his pen & the ringmaster's
bleeding, thick black blood center stage. I'm light-years

from recovery, tailbone-digging science lab, sun
crystallizing test tubes flowering near eye-washing
stations, blistering visions that I'm still the school slut. Everyone

said so. Only my mama wouldn't believe it. Nor Einstein.
I imagine he never sent Lieserl to live on a farm with family—they say
she was mentally slow & died of scarlet fever as a baby.

But I believe she lived.

                                        Tonight I'm leaving
for the circus. Tonight I'm dreaming myself a star.

LIESERL READS GOODNIGHT MOON

I like to think the moon is there even if I am not looking at it.
—ALBERT EINSTEIN, *ON QUANTUM INDETERMINACY*

I like to think that you are here, Rosa, though you're clearly gone. Look—
pajamas on my dresser where you left them. Plain as the yellow-checkered day.

I like to think that I'm still a good person.

I like to think I can eat the world in chocolate cake, whole bags of flour mixed
with water, become a dough baby & eat myself in dough, & nothing will change,
not my cheeks or my stomach or the way you look at me.

I like to think that my father did not abandon me.

There is an answer for the blank-faced clock that takes everything away, that
cuckoo clucking, *Why bother building bridges? Don't you know this all is ending soon?*

I like to think that cuckoo's deluded. But then I hear myself, ticking . . .

I like to think that night's the same as the day, only darker. The moon has a pen-
chant for drama. She *shimmers.*

I like to think you're still here. The way the moon disappears in her game of hide
& seek where she's not spiraling but changing costumes or drinking gin. The
moon drinks gin. Yes—

I like to think that.

LIESERL WRITES HER FATHER

"I am very sorry about what has happened to Lieserl. Scarlet fever often leaves some lasting trace behind."
—ALBERT EINSTEIN, *LETTER TO MILEVA MARIĆ*

Is there no peace in this world
my dearest father's father, my dearest yellow, yes.

I am alone; her wounds crawl into my dress
of skin, of honeyed straw, of starched white lab coats.

Still a mystery, your *radical new ideas about time*
or the illegitimate child devastating sun & moon

white with fever. What daughter you left to no
body, I've become—chasing elevators & bending light

like sky so blue so water stagnant in a bowl, these root
years. If I am not careful, we will never again

exist. We're moving & so fast. Ink splotches
in a dog's dreams. Did you know that dogs also dream?

Night comes. Einstein, night. Our meridian slides
another reddish leaf on the tablecloth & loose at the stitches

like the girl whose name meant small-winged one.
Lieserl lost as choking hearts of the death flower, her daemon

in the coal-burning stove that almost killed you.
Our fates knitted to *the secular saint who solved*

geometry problems for little girls then wept over
the destruction of cherry-blossomed cities.

NIEVE, THE BRAVE SISTER

More than just *watching* street performers
eat their fire or waste their bodies

enduring their own art
Nieve *understands* their tricks   She climbs

inside their tanks
sidling their wet-suit bodies

in nothing but her slips
then clasps her hands around her silver hair

& holds her icy breath
the longest   They marvel   like they've never

witnessed miracle girls before
though Nieve swears   we're everywhere

When she emerges   blue & shimmering
I offer her my jacket   a slice of jellied bread

fearing how she does not need
how she does not need *me.*

ROSA/NIEVE'S SIDESHOW
PERFORMANCE

Like the two-headed baby in the circus jar
        arms curled around themselves so
around each other   in utero   in glass

& twinned   always
        conjoined in ditchwater
though our mama gave us separate

births   canal into which we sink
        like the hull of a ship
nightly welcomes us   home

is memory's circus
        swimming
a billowing tent   on display

the woman swallowing knives
        the man who claims the pain   needling
his cheek flesh pads

makes him feel
        alive   we twins who are twins
only in this shadowed spectacle

keep diving headfirst into the water
        not deep enough for river

for irrigating sugar beets   for searing
        granules sweet on the tongue
unbroken

twins but for the roots
            of our fingernails as we wait each night
to arrive   mud pickling our eyes.

LIESERL'S YELLOW

What I'm searching for, Father,
what I'm trying to tell you in my simple way:
you spoke in the language of mathematics
beautifully precise—& I never spoke at all
beyond the sounds babies make for pleasure
but these like soft, round toes or grubby fingers
so full of life—

Remember how I pulled you off the couch
& your head hit the floor when the coal-burning
stove would have killed you?

They say it was your friend Zangger
but it was your little ghost of a girl
you must have known all along for you said:
Put your hand on a hot stove for a minute,
it seems like an hour. Sit with a pretty girl for an hour,
it seems like a minute. That's relativity.

It's an act of peace, communicating with the dead—
yellow against yellow.

I've become a periodic
table of elemental disasters
flowering despite the last frost
                    before spring, come too soon.

LIESERL CREATES LIGHT

I tell my children there's nothing in the dark that isn't there in the light.
Light energy triggers a molecular dance that allows us to distinguish
the shadows—
edges of objects, of faces, a mallard duck in a pond or a paper cup
de café con leche.
What breaks this ordinary experience?
The feeling that I cannot believe the data?

I tell my children we are gifts.
Light is a gift.

ROSA & THE DATE PALM

Come find me under the black persimmon tree   Nieve
where prayers bear wrinkled fruit   bear messages home

come tend me at sunrise   like sweeping
a grave   offering fresh tortillas

rolled each morning   menudo steaming on the stove
My patch of yellowing in the grass   my lungs culling holes

in the sweet so close to my palms I can nearly grasp
What does a mouth hold but secrets   What tongue in mine

What bone-handled crotch & tissue paper wadded to staunch
the bleeding   The boy on the bicycle called my name   pulled

it from my mouth like meat from the seed &
his older brother with a truck   A hole in the floorboard

A hole in the world
                              Persimmons call themselves stories

of the gods   Nieve   did you also wake into the mythical
I mean   rise yourself   hold the cast of yourself

bones splitting as moonstones   as midnight   undone
Leaves fall across my eyes   Nieve   come find me before I bloom.

AFTER THE CIRCUS

Someone stuck a doorknob on an empty
nail protruding from a staircase.
Not a knob, exactly, but a child safety
doorknob cover, grip & twist, white & skeletal,
like the exoskeleton of a doorknob
where there was no door.

It reminded me of the oryx horn
the ringmaster bored into the small
goat's forehead for the sideshow act:
the boot-chewing unicorn I came
to love in the left ring.
I opened the door.

It's temporary music, called the one
I believed responsible for
the doorless knob. The music:
tinny goat bleating, only it came
from a sleek-maned creature
whose lone horn was real.

I meant to ask how being there
was possible & how many others
but when I opened my mouth
I released bright yellow
birds carrying umbrellas
like coltsfoot with wings.

I flooded the sky with flowers;
they rained for a hundred days,
& when they landed, I mounted
my small love grown tall, my wounded

one grown strong. We rode
through yellow fields as vast & open

as doors.

THREE

ROSA MEETS PRINCESS ALICE

after Jesse Bering

When I was young I fell in love with the Scientist
        who came to my school, rounded kids up at random
& introduced us to Princess Alice.

He pointed toward an empty chair
        It isn't empty. She's really there.
She would speak to those who believed.

She came to love us, Princess Alice.
        We brought her boxes of chocolate orange
peels & fat purple artichokes.

The Scientist asked questions, then watched
        how we'd respond. We didn't know
he was recording from a camera in the corner—

we only knew to throw darts at the impossible
        target from behind our backs
without cheating because Princess Alice

was watching from her invisible throne.
        There was another group, I found out later,
who did not receive the gift of Princess Alice—

who felt no presence in the inexplicable, who crossed
        the line taped to the ground, then turned
around or set the dart straight in the bull's-eye,

who spent their love on something tangible.
        & although the test confirmed we are merely
wired to believe

I loved him for offering
        our small hearts
to someone only we could see.

WHY BELIEVE? OR, ROSA QUESTIONS THE SCIENTIST ABOUT THE PRINCESS

The Scientist first met Princess Alice
when his mama died. His sadness
was the color of gunmetal boats,
shaped like a broom handle.

He wasn't watching for signs.
He didn't believe in that. A scientist
believes only the data. & only as long
as it can be reproduced.

Still, she came in the form of wind chimes
on the back porch where there was no wind.
There must have been wind, I said—
once I'd finally figured it all out

or at least once I'd thought I had.
                    No, it was a windless evening.

Yet the clinking began—like tiny forks
against ceramic plates, tiny platters in sinks.
Test tubes in sinks, I said, my toes curled
between his bare thighs.

                    My father had gone away
                    on his great science experiment.

(That's how I labeled & stored it away
for safekeeping in the alphabetized
catalog of my girlhood.)

The Scientist's grant took him to the river—

from its icy beginning in southern Colorado
to Albuquerque through Socorro, down
to Las Cruces & finally to its grisly end—
its mouth forever opening into Mexico's gullet.

　　　　　　　How sad, the river is never able
to shut herself—

He called me his Great Monarch, building
myself a chrysalis wherever I needed.

Had he replaced the Princess? In truth
I cannot always remember what I believed.
Or when.

AFTER MEETING PRINCESS ALICE

The year Father left for his science project
Mama began wearing to Mass a white veil over her hair
embarrassing me (it looks like she's wearing
a coffee table doily on her head)—& she calls
me tonta with my cone-shaped party hats on the back porch
waiting for Father's return.

Sometimes I put the cone in front of my face
like a medieval plague mask
or a toucan beak.
The crows in Leonora Carrington's *Bird Bath*
I saw when Father took me to Mexico City to watch her painting.

Mama slaps my face when I lie.
I imagine the birthmark on my neck grows redder
with each fresh slap. Soon my whole body will be red.
They'll rename me Roja
& I'll wear my new pain like skin.

ROSA FOLLOWS LIESERL INTO NIGHT

I pray to the Princess
my boxes of juggling balls
in silver & white
weighing at my conscience—

She has not answered since nightfall
when I asked her if I should run.

Go, I heard in the wind chimes
at Mama's back porch.

       Go now.

               In her desert I'm thirsty.
I've forgotten my lunch box & canteen.
I've forgotten myself like a pair of preteen
& period-stained chones in the locker room trash can.

The strawberry birthmark
on my neck? Mama says
I was kissed by God.
I wonder what ice cream tastes like
in heaven.

In a growl like mountain lions:
Why are you here, child?

& the answer is Nieve.

PRINCESS ALICE RESPONDS

There's a kind of grace in the children who believe in me most—
their prayers, simplest. Without frills.

They come with hands on boxes, asking which holds the ball.
I flicker switches.

The youngest cannot understand the connection.
The older ones believe they've already failed.

This is love, no? This is God.

LIESERL CONTEMPLATES RESURRECTION

I believe in the conservation
of bird wings, in tiny packages of light

& their insistence on shining
in the resurrection of dying things.

But even if we could take the DNA
from Einstein's white hair & clone him, implant

him in my sponge-red uterus then guard me
till I emit him screaming from between my legs

pinning hopes that now he'd finally understand
how *spooky action at a distance* is real

& this time around we would keep time

whether or not it existed, still, he could not grow up
into the man I need him to be—

THE DEAD DON'T CRICK.
THE DEAD BELIEVE

in swallowing feathers

I once read in the news   a little girl
with an itch at her throat   scratched & scratched
until a quicksilver-slick feather broke through her skin
needling like a profane birthmark

When I died   I felt a birthday party in my brain
they were here for me
the guests   the universe convening
to expand & fade away
a piñata strung

               atop the highest star

Mama was not always dead

            she was once perfectly living
with fingernail polish & a ribboned

headband like a gunboat-gray tiara
for keeping hair from forehead

O god
of party   nightfall fiesta
& the matter of hearts   livers   kidneys stomachs synapses

neurons   eyes
launching spectacular hallucinations
blowing

          out the candles on the human body of a cake

(I felt a funeral in my brain)

                                     O god of lighting candles
O god like light   & light the fastest means
of letting go *(I feel it glowing in my bones)*

FOUR

ROSA'S TIME CAPSULE (OR, FATHER IS A HOLE & HOME, A SPINNING TOP)

Father believed he'd invented
        a forgetting machine

We spent the soundtrack of my childhood
working on it together

       tick, tick, tick   Songbirds
thwacked themselves against windowpanes

in a house fire
       1971   Alan Shepard left three golf balls

on the moon   Father flung his golf club
into a tree when he was in a tournament

      & losing   The earth seen from the moon
reminds us of the phases

we went through
      together, *tick, tick*   Rebellious teenager

with her drunk father   Poet seeking
redemption & her Catholic ascetic   He's turned

      careful in his old age
leaving his ghost

prints on paper-white gurneys   a hole ticking
      in his daughter's memory
                From any spot

on the absent-minded moon
the earth inhabits the sky-same place

        a wasted father
pissing in the bed he shared with Mama

my baby dolls
        splintered to the pockmarked walls

Tick   I launch these off
on their gold-anodized plaques   where they'll

        catch up with both *Voyagers*
then explode.

RISEN AGAIN

Anything can be a time machine.
For us it was the elms grown crooked
into each other, knobby rooted
& shooting nine stories into the sky.
I named one Risen Again
for how it branched down into dirt
then up again, snakelike, hiding places
for me & the others. But it transported only me—
& Nieve. We could disappear
into its corkscrewed trunk & be two
places at once, for I'd found a way to split
myself. What the grown-ups didn't know:
enough to dredge the river
cemetery where we'd play hide & seek
& never find. Enough to send us
where they no longer existed.
But the boy the color of an oak casket who
guarded me in the tree's clearing so I could cross
would no more make it to adulthood
than any of us. I knew that about him
& loved him anyway. What did it feel like, splitting?
Like ice pops against summer heat
bare feet scalding asphalt & eggs dropping
on sidewalk to test a theory. We fried
ourselves like sizzling pork fat plucked
from the comal & dipped in chile.
We held our whole bodies like a tree
after anyone had tried to chop it down.
A time machine can be anything
can be one's own body. I used to catch rattlers
in the foothills for five bucks a snake.
I'd leash each snake's neck so it couldn't strike

then pinch between gloved fingers into a bag
for the exotic-animal collector next door.
Splitting felt like that, like catching
but also getting caught. Whichever way I twisted
felt like shedding skin, felt too tight.
Whichever way I turned felt like out.

ACCELERATING ELEVATOR

Are they rising or falling? Rosa & Nieve
cannot determine the way things fall, even
when they expect the drop, the impossible
thought experiment: to be in a box

in space away from globes or suns
no stars whirring past
to show movement or stillness—
Are they frozen? Lurching

in the peach pits of small stomachs?
I'm dizzy, Rosa tells her sister. Maybe
schizophrenia works this way—how it's
impossible for two people in two different

frames of reference to agree on the time.
Gravity works this way too, with our eyes closed
or the windows shut. *I've just had the happiest thought*
Nieve says, the ice of her hair melting rapidly

at these speeds— *A girl falling is the same as flying
downward.* Einstein said similar, & there was no
soft pile of garbage the way the media got it all
wrong, how Newton's apple never landed

on his head. *Watch the light, Nieve—*
It curls, & she's not sure why
bending was predicted. Nothing's
pulling. Toward whom is the body floating &

what happens in the elevator?
One of the sisters inevitably presses a button
to stop the flow—

Cállate, Nieve. Quarry men are climbing the cliffs,
their drunken deserts. Let's pretend instead it's
Stephen Hawking in his wheelchaired throne
or David Blaine come to show us how endurance

is an art, like everything else, like dying. When
Nieve goes with David to the underwater tank
& pulls needles through her palm, narrowly
missing bone, Rosa wonders how

she ever survived childhood, crawling
these caves—she begins missing
her family, the way Lieserl wanders
in her fevered dreams, each girl lonely

as a single particle can ever be, connected
to every piece of light/matter there ever was
both spooky & translucent.
The elevator crashes. There is no elevator.

HOW TO BUILD A TIME MACHINE

Mama—
spread your legs & let the daughter

out. She will survive you, she will
carry your messed-up genes

into a future you're unwilling
to imagine.

Close your eyes & imagine
your daughter becoming the light

becoming godlike
in her indifference.

                              Mama,

we are a brilliant machine—

CASE STUDY: THE MEXICALI BORDER AS TIME MACHINE

I crossed over
for cumbia for tequila

& holy water, fearful
serpent, my feathered scales

like marigolds
altar spilled like sugar in a sideshow

only there was no circus, no
last act, & I can't tell a story without

breaking. Border crosser,
rosary holder,

communion starched of want,
bread stale in the mouth,

one woman held out the heavy
basket of her hands,

turnpike bloody.
I was young & slipping

into splatter, taco cart of cilantro
& lime. Border-crossing women—

we've been no fence
& empty hinges.

REINAS DE STEM

"Not only are Latinas recognized for being super sexy, but they're also extremely smart. Here are just a few recognized in science and more."
    —*LATIN TIMES*

Mama shapes masa into hypodermic needle
Mama shapes lump of clay & calls it my pudgy nose my pudgy face
Nursing bag is dangerously low of diabetes meds
Google says I must be sexy
less sugar more injection
Lydia Villa-Komaroff helped make those sugar sticks
I need when my blood is burning spun sugar
Mija look into the mirror at those lonjas
You're getting fat, & no one wants a chubby princess
to be a STEM queen like Adriana Ocampo
planetary geologist at NASA
or the face that launched the Chicxulub among the Mayan ruins
& set even prehistoric beasts afire
Mama's chupacabra stainless steel & the biologist says, *Women are not socialized*
to believe
they can earn a living much less be
a scientist—   But France Anne-Dominic Córdova at Los Alamos
of rays both X & gamma is no pageant sovereign
& Ellen Ochoa (Xicana tearing choke weed breaking branches stem by stem)
flew in space
Mama look at me look at me
                    I float   I fly

NIEVE EXPLORA

Rosa & I've found a new habitable planet.
Like in Chagall's *Lovers* the first perpetual
night. We read in a pop-up children's book
that dinosaurs may have suffered
depression—like how I know I need her
here. We're a vanishing dinosaur species.
We pretend we're teachers. Telescopes
track the orbit our stars make across night—
we wave good-bye. Do you remember your first
sunrise? Your first kiss in a humid
gymnasium? Remember the first words
you never say, that cannot undo the train
you were riding from somewhere but can't
remember which city & you're still whirling
past cow fields & fiddleheads? The book says
maybe that's how the dinosaurs went—
it wasn't a rock on fire but a massive
sadness. We turn away, pointing out the earth:
first women to float like lovers. First daughters
to save their fathers. First sisters even space
                    never got.

ROSA DREAMS OF NOTHING

What I heard while drifting toward sleep—
dark matter is the scaffolding of our universe.

Cosmologists know it only by its white glowing
against the red of our familiar matter,

the skin against our cheekbones, our lips
against ceramic coffee mugs, each other's lips,

& while I slept I dreamt of icebergs
massive in the nothingness surrounding us,

& while I dreamt, the Scientist felt far away
washing bodies in the hospital, sewing skin

back to skin across the wounded planets.
We need that beautiful nothing, that skeletal

emptiness we know must be there—
for it holds us. For it holds us together.

GHOST YOU DON'T BELIEVE IN

Richard Feynman's wife Arline died within a few weeks of Hiroshima.
—"LOVE & THE BOMB," IN *NO ORDINARY GENIUS*

The world looks so different after learning science.
—RICHARD FEYNMAN

I've bled the night's silence
like wild ginger, determined to believe we are alive

always & death is merely a rearrangement
of atoms, the way your Arline left you

weeks after Hiroshima, not because she stopped
believing you were a good man but because

her body was not enough.   The clock
stopped when she died, & you thought your love turned

peculiar, a ghost you didn't believe in, haunting you
from the skepticism of your own science-hardened heart.

I am so tired of not believing. It's exhausting,
all these particles of thought, little packets of questions

ripping in the mind—   Won't you draw me
from the maps of our neurons?

Find me in the lines between what we know
we cannot prove—our *spooky action*

at a distance, all the quantum of our boundary-
breaking love.

NIEVE AFTER THE CIRCUS, PARALLEL

Rosa, the coffin had a hole—

I saw you through the ground
                              & there we were
in Risen Again—stranger than

                    sisters—you wormhole, you death
kisser, Einstein girl in your circus tent—
come home to me.
                              This is the year

of wonders. This is the year I stay
                    alive. The world again
in the urgent care.

                    The Princess says she talks to your younger self
convincing you/her not to press wrist
                    against blade (you stopped yourself/her once).

If the world is ending, then we
                              bottle earthquakes, we
ice storm over the crackling river

                    (the dying orange leaves) of the body.

ROSA & NIEVE SAY GOOD-BYE TO THE DESERT CIRCUS

Unbloom the night cactus   return
honey bats to their nocturne roost

empty the prickling organ pipes   refill
every minc

Bodies in motion must
for every girl with nectar in her mouth
for every sister filled with fruit

Deworm   recap
restrain   Unpollinate
the desert   unslake its stubborn ventricles

skull-white   bone-dry
girl-empty

                    Within the fever
We compose one elegant equation
one simple prayer

recant the forward flow of time   unmouth
the dirge   unchant good-bye
unbury the child   unbury

the child   (the backyard
hasn't looked this safe in years) unswallow the sky

Break its beak   its brittle arrow
unslung   rock-split

                    There is a way back.

FIVE

FROM THE BOTTOM OF THE WORLD COMES A CRY

then Death has her day—she sings in tones
we recognize as the road.

                            Remember

the first road we marked as the one out of town, Nieve?

Wake up, Sister. We're drowning.

Cores finely decorated in boxwood:
an apple falls from a tree & hits
a scientist in the head—apocryphal,

how we're his daughters. You of the fair skin,
& I, with the red bite mark on my neck.
(We come alive, we come undone.)

In the thought experiment of the cave,
we're supposed to *choose* who's allowed to live—

Time is like a river

                            & we're sitting along its edge
eating bowls of sweet nopales with red rice.

ROSA & NIEVE GROW UP

In the last battle the unicorn bloodies her horn.

Past the bosque marshlands she must
suffer. Her hooves are meant for loam.

                                         Listen, nights
bloom jasmine from the salt bones, our rib cages

sprouting like burial plots. Her myth
unburies us. How we've flanked her with handprints—

reddest for love. She isn't girlhood-breaking.
She isn't imagination-must-fail.
                                When we were children

something unbearable. In the last battle
we kept what belonged, what came into this world

with us—we became a woman like this:
                           the blood was mine the blood
was mine the blood. Nieve rides back into memory.

THE WORLD ENDED.
I WOKE IN HEAVEN

as Nieve your sister white as snow
I'd abandoned you as all gods—I wasn't

real, darling. Think of me, fondly.
Though I wasn't real. My daughter Lieserl

says real is when it can speak.
She & I are real, the dog is real.

How does the dog speak, I ask,
& Lieserl barks. *The computer is real*

because listen—she sets Pandora playing.

SIGHTING

Last night in the backyard   your shawl
flung across the swing set   I found you

gnawing carrots from Mama's garden
with such a simple grace I believed

that moment you were a white rabbit
a sweet phantom animal come to lead

me somewhere strange   Moonlight greased
the mountain ranges surrounding us

gunmetal gray & fettering us to this home
we once shared   Nieve   sister new as snow

returned like the red rash on my neck
may I ask your blessing to stay?

Will you answer me? Surely those aren't worms
chafing your eyes   Not your shucked

remains littering Mama's soil   Slotted
between hedgerows you remind me what you mean

a glimpse into the other/world is enough
(you haven't left me   alone)

RIVER PITCH; OR, NIEVE REMINDS ME HOW TO SWIM

You fractured your hip bone
falling for a boy who danced
you into thirteen jagged pieces, lace
tunic over leggings, the lank trunk
of your newly teenaged body fast-pitching
you forward, as if trying to ruin
each fine & breakable thing, the ruins
of your body's handiwork, reduced to bone
shards. *No,* Mama said when you pitched
a fit (she couldn't be left alone)— *Dance*
in my living room.

                        You'd plumbed her attic trunk
of moth-chewed costumes, lining the lace
of her wedding dress against the laced
bobbin of her old sewing machine, ruining
both, your zigzag stitches like rings in a trunk,
attaching branches of bodice, boned
at the buds of your breasts, sudden twins dancing
across your chest ready to pitch
you through the bathroom window into pitch-
black night with the boy who'd interlace
them, promising your first dance
but first, who'd stop at the bosque to ruin
a bottle of his father's wine, bone-
dry under a blanket in the trunk.

How did you end in a river, his boxers for trunks,
your skin for a bathing suit, the pitch
of your voices & the waves echoing a boned-
hollow of the absent music, laced

with regret? *I'll make up for ruining*
your night, he'd said. *Let's dance*
here, in the water, like Baby in Dirty Dancing.

Once, you read someone found in a tree trunk
a set of human teeth while mining the ruined
coast after a hurricane. The pitch
of a quarry is the softest place—
its density of childhood bones,
corkscrew bones, forks in a river dancing
as a boy laces a willing trunk
with the pitch & fury of rock toward ruin.

NIGHT AFTER NIGHT: JUPITER

Skoll the wolf god lived in the sky
& sometimes ate the sun.

If the laws of nature are fixed
what role is there for God?

Three tiny dots beside Jupiter
& then a fourth dot appeared

Galileo watching in wonder
these moons circling

proof positive that at least some objects
do not orbit the earth.

(I know the science of eclipse
but still I need the wolf.)

Consider the man who wants to build a hill
on a flat piece of land.

To make this hill, he digs a hole
& uses the soil.

But he's not just making a hill.
He's making a hole—

The hill's a negative
(we begin at zero)

& the wolf is hunger.   Night
after night, I watch him eat. Proof positive

at least one girl can fix herself

        from that whole scorching sky.

BODY IMAGE; OR, NIEVE REMINDS ME WHO I AM

If the earth were flat
        you could spot a candle flickering
        from thirty miles away.

When you blush
        the lining of your stomach
        blushes too.

You contain more atoms
        than stars in our galaxy.

Thousands of years ago
        you ran after prey
        until it died of exhaustion.

You could run for that long.

Each hour
        you release enough heat
        to boil water.

A block of your bone
        just a matchbox of your bone
        could support
        nine elephants.

You are bioluminescent.
You glow in the dark—

If you could pick up the light
                    with your illusionist's eyes
                    you would see
                    who you are—

You would see who you are
                    & marvel.

WHY ARE YOU IN THIS WORLD?—

the speaker again.
Empty your skirts on the table
lay your burdens down
before the X-ray
metal detectors & pickpockets.
Father is a scientist, I tell them
& Mama, a devout.
Devout what?
The speaker will not relent.
I must account.
We meet mouth to probe.
The light fastening my rib cage
bounces jumbled through another wormhole
in my throat.
O holy day.
I am born.
Here I will not let go.
Nieve bears herself to my side.
The speaker opens eyeholes.
Keys jangle.
There is hope.
We slide again, two girls, two slats in the face of the break.
We've come breathing.
We've come ready to live again.

MY GOD, NIEVE

My god at the laundromat says her washing machine works but
the power's out so she's been drying it on the line. My god

waits in line at the WIC counter to weigh her kids, account
for their eating habits, check the box for *no*

they're not eating mud or lead or other poisons
and *yes* she gets it: her choices are dry *or* canned beans

or peanut butter. My god's not allergic to peanut butter, likes
the creaminess gumming her bread-mouth,

her ten-dollars-worth of fresh *or* frozen veggie coupons.
On a dare, at fourteen, my god stole a carton

of Thrifty's Rocky Road, tried convincing the store manager
she was pregnant under her Sally dress, but got so cold,

my god, she dropped the box right there in the aisle,
grateful she got caught. Now the cashier pays my god

veggie change in cash, so she buys each kid a cone. My god
is frozen-mouth. She is get-out-of-this-town-

or-hell-freezes-over. She is paycheck
to paycheck. Each night when she goes to bed, my god

kisses her kids' clean faces, then, thanking herself, her own.

ROSA & NIEVE IN THE BEGINNING

1. ROSA

The balloon animals wilting in the city's
zoo remind me. When I turn
circus, I wear more than costume.

Girl whose mama locks
herself in for days. Girl
whose potions

fail, her fingers muddying
leaves & earthworms.
The mama goes out

of focus with her heft & weight.
In her hands, cold tortillas.
She calls me cochina. Dirty girl.

Pig child. I tug at my basalt-
black hair, braided
with colorful ribbons Mama

fixes each morning
because it soothes her nerves
to comb & brush & smooth.

She leaves on my face
handprinted splotches redder
than the strawberry

birthmark on my neck.

2. NIEVE

When I was young, my white grandma gave me
a book of famous women, women who'd done something—

it took many years before I noticed not one of those women
was Latina. I decided then I would be a poet.

She gave me *A Brief History of Time* the year she gave me a letter
begging me to end it with my sister's no-good boyfriend. A decade later

I'd married, had three kids, & written a novel
about how insane I was back then. I could bottle

the crazy that way. Only maybe I didn't put it that way
in the book. I blamed Rosa. *Corazón da esperanza de nada.*

The heart holds out in the prospect of nothing. Thirty-three years
on this earth, & it's worse than ever. No Latina has won

the Pulitzer Prize for poetry. I'm living in the ashes of the Cristo
candles Mama gave me. I want to erase this. I'm fighting

with my fingers against the keyboard, my pinky inching
toward the backspace arrow, just a few spaces away, across

the *p* the brackets the back dash (how often have I sprinted
toward the exit? I was on the phone with the airline,

almost canceling my New England artist's retreat).
One teacher advised I write to someone in another country

in another time in another language, as if my words might
end up in some Argentinian Cueva de las Manos, syllables

like henna-stained handprints, like my ex's on my nalgas.
Risen Again wasn't like Narnia. There was no other realm—

there is only this universe, but it is wondrous strange.
Inside the trunk was a mirror. I saw myself in there.

I could back & forth a while. & then I got stuck.
I didn't mean to break the glass.

                                        I was Rosa.

Then & now.

3. ROSA

No one believed me when I told them
about the mirror. It didn't have to be a mirror.

In some girls' rooms, I'd heard rumors
it was a book. A dollhouse. A painting—
could dislocate a self from a body.

We unstuck in time—but it's more than that.

It's not that some people are unstuck in time.
Some people are unstuck from their own lives.

Unstuck from what they love. Unstuck from themselves.

They are & aren't themselves. They are & aren't
real. & that's the problem. Lacan's mirror is real.
Emily Dickinson said something like, *I am afraid to own*

a Body— / a small domain, a coffin—

4. NIEVE

The monsoons come all summer, drowning
the grasshoppers winged & mothlike swarming
into the city from the desert edges all drought-ridden
spring. Mamas warn their children not

to squash them with their chanclas or, worse,
their bare feet—not to catch & bottle them
with leaves to eat & a napkin covering the lid
because a life contained in the hands of a greed-

curious child large as a giant or a monster
in comparison, large enough to murder entire
nations of grasshoppers, is no life at all. Still,
when the mountain ranges in the distance

begin covering themselves with thick, fawn-
colored clouds & lightning crackles the sky,
even the grasshoppers must understand
their time is nearing its end.

5. THE PRINCESS

(It was a fool's journey from the beginning,
but I've told you that already.)

She braided her mama's history like myth
into her ribboned hair. Sunrise tinged

the desert lemon merengue, & Rosa wondered
how long their snacks would suffice. She thought
of pink sugar melting on the lawn, only

there was no lawn in the desert—
　　　　　　　Rosa felt a scratching in her throat all morning.
　　　　　　　Maybe it's a swallow that'll grow red wings & fly away.

In the desert, the girls found unlimited potential
for catastrophe or miracle.
                     That morning before the sun rose twice, Rosa woke

& decided that had to be the beginning—
her whole arching solstice quieted like the first twig in spring
sags at its branch from the never-ending cold.

She picked at the scab on her neck
but there was no goldenrod, & it didn't sting the way of nettle
in her stomach or the glowing science stick.

The sprig in her throat spindling, she dreamt
that quilts laid out an altar with a sign: G$.

She named this nothing, but he came as light against glass.
She didn't know his voice until he spoke

& then she remembered the Scientist.

G$

               With a flashlight under the covers
she stays up late each night reading
                          Einstein & Gödel, time bandits.

It's not that Rosa's afraid anyone will come &
make her stop reading (her mama never even gets out of bed).

It's just that she feels less alone this way—
The universe expanding but also rotating

like a Ferris wheel, spinning us all
a kind of circus

in our brief & fiery deserts.

ACKNOWLEDGMENTS

Gratitude and love to my poetry sisters, ever lighting my dark trek through the desert: Alicia Elkort (rejoicer of all things girl power), Avra Elliott (my own Nieve in the wilds of New Mexico), Stacey Balkun (curator of all things magical and mythic), Stephanie Bryant Anderson (keeper of the light and all the dark and lovely bones it holds), and Nandini Dhar (comrade brave and true). To my beautiful first editors of this collection, Jeannine Hall Gailey and Kelly Davio, who believed in the heroic journey of Rosa y Nieve. To Andrew for wandering through Los Alamos with me and the archives of every library and museum and for watching every single episode of *Through the Wormhole* with me and for listening to all my excited stories of physicists and magicians and black holes and how these were the key to saving my own soul. To Van Jordan for showing me Mileva Marić in his *Quantum Lyrics*, the knowledge of whose existence led me to Lieserl, little flower and the heart of this whole project. To my mother and daughter. To my own slightly mad scientist father. Thank you.

Thank you also to the wonderful editors of the journals in which the following poems previously appeared:

Blue Mesa Review: "When the Jornada del Muerto Had a Windpipe" (2014 Poetry Prize second-place winner; included in the *2015 Best of the Net Anthology*)

Cultural Weekly: "Lieserl Travels Back to the River, Becomes Her Mama"

Drunk Monkey: "Accelerating Elevator," "Lieserl Runs Away"

Indiana Review: "My God, Nieve" (2015 Poetry Prize runner-up)

KROnline: "Lieserl Contemplates Resurrection"

Life and Legends: "Sighting"

Madison Review: "Rosa & Nieve Say Good-bye to the Desert Circus" (previously titled "Reverse: A Girlhood"; 2015 Poetry Prize finalist)

Mas Tequila Review: "Un Niño, Falling"

Passages North: "Rosa Follows Nieve into the Desert Circus" (previously titled "Nieve in the Desert Circus"; 2015 Elinor Benedict Poetry Prize finalist)

Prairie Schooner: "Lunatic Mama: The Last Hunger Artist"

Scissors & Spackle: "Rosa Meets Princess Alice"

Tinderbox Poetry Journal: "River Pitch; or, Nieve Reminds Me How to Swim"

Zone 3: "The Bomb," "In the Desert Multiverse: Einstein's Single Mama," "Night After Night: Jupiter"

NOTES

Rosa Roja as well as **Rosa & Nieve in the Beginning** & other poems take some of their information about Kurt Gödel & Albert Einstein from Jim Holt's article "Time Bandits: What Were Einstein & Gödel Talking About?" (*New Yorker*, 2005). According to Holt, "Kurt Gödel, often called the greatest logician since Aristotle, was a strange & ultimately tragic man, who subsisted on a valetudinarian's diet of butter, baby food, & laxatives. He had a tendency toward paranoia, believed in ghosts; he had a morbid dread of being poisoned by refrigerator gases; he refused to go out when certain distinguished mathematicians were in town, apparently out of concern that they might try to kill him. 'Every chaos is a wrong appearance,' he insisted—the paranoiac's first axiom." He died of starvation after refusing to eat.

The Bomb cites information from *The Day the Sun Rose Twice* by Ferenc Morton Szasz (1984).

Lieserl Writes Her Father cites information from "Einstein's Lost Child" by Frederic Golden (*TIME*, 1999). Mileva Marić gave birth to Einstein's first child, a daughter, before they married. According to Golden, "The illegitimate child in Einstein's past did not come to light until more than 30 years after his death, when the first volume of his collected papers finally appeared, in 1987." Scholars believe that Marić gave Lieserl to her parents & that she died in infancy of scarlet fever. Whether or not this was her true fate remains a mystery.

Rosa Meets Princess Alice & other poems cite information from "Did We Invent God," an episode of *Through the Wormhole* (directed by James Younger, written by Anthony Lund, 2012).

Lieserl Contemplates Resurrection & **Ghost You Don't Believe In**: The phrase "spooky action at a distance" is a direct quote from Einstein regarding his belief that quantum theory is unbelievable.

Nieve Explora is inspired by Christa McAuliffe, the first American teacher scheduled to fly into space, who died in the *Challenger* space shuttle explosion; she wrote, "I cannot join the space program & restart my life as an astronaut, but this opportunity to connect my abilities with my interests in history & space is a unique opportunity to fulfill my early fantasies."

Ghost You Don't Believe In reimagines the relationship between Nobel Prize–winning physicist Richard Feynman & his wife, Arline, who died of tuberculosis shortly after Feynman completed his work on the nuclear bombs created in Los Alamos & launched during World War II. When she died at 9:21 p.m., the clock in her room stopped (*No Ordinary Genius* by Richard Feynman and Christopher Sykes, 1996).

From the Bottom of the World Comes a Cry: Italics quote Stephen Hawking from "How to Build a Time Machine" (*Daily Mail* [UK], 2010).

Many poems are inspired by Stephen Hawking's *A Brief History of Time* (1988).

ABOUT THE AUTHOR

Jennifer Givhan is a Mexican American writer and activist from the Southwestern desert and the author of three previous full-length poetry collections: *Landscape with Headless Mama* (2015 Pleiades Editors' Prize), *Protection Spell* (2016 Miller Williams Poetry Series), and *Girl with Death Mask* (2017 Blue Light Books Prize, selected by Ross Gay). Her honors include a National Endowment for the Arts Creative Writing Fellowship, PEN America's Emerging Voices Fellowship, the Frost Place Latin@ Scholarship, a National Latino Writers' Conference scholarship, the *Lascaux Review* Poetry Prize, *Phoebe Journal*'s Greg Grummer Poetry Prize, and the Pinch Poetry Prize.